The Splendour of
WINDSOR

ETON, HAMPTON COURT AND LEGOLAND

160 COLOUR ILLUSTRATIONS - 11 MAPS

Victoria Memorial and Windsor Castle.

(P. 2/3) Windsor's Castle. Air View.

Cover:
Windsor's Castle. Air View.

THOMAS BENACCI LTD
LONDON

St. George's Chapel. Main stairs entrance.

Hampton Court Palace. South Facade.

Guildhall.

Long Walk.

Legoland. Tower Bridge.

Eton College.

SOUTH MEADOW LANE

A·332 RELIEF ROAD

RECREATION GROUND

SOUTH MEA

MEA

BIRD SANCTUARY

RIVER THAME

TH

Clewer St. Andrew

WINDSOR LEISURE CENTRE

PLEASURE GARDENS

P

STOVELL RD.

BARRY AVENUE

BA

CLEWER PARK

MILL LANE

CLEWER

STEPHENSN DR.

ROAD

Clewer St. Stephen

P

CLEWER VILLAGE

PLAYING FIELD

DUKE STREET

VANSITTART RD.

VANSITTART INDUSTRIAL ESTATE

A·308

PAV.

MAIDENHEAD RD.

ARTHUR

ROAD

PARSONAGE LANE

RECTORY CL.

THE WINDSOR BOYS SCHOOL

OXFORD ROAD

CLEWER FIELDS

ALMA ROAD

ORCHARD AV.

ALBERT STREET

BEXLEY STREET

CLA

OLD PEOPLES CENTRE

CLARENCE ROAD

DORSET RD

CLARENCE RD.

FAWCETT RD.

Clewer Within

CLAREMO

CLEWER NEW TOWN

GREEN

CLEWER AVENUE

VANSITTART RECREATION GROUND

VANSITTART RD.

MUNICIPAL OFFICES

EAST BERKSH COLLE

Clewer New Town

GOSLAR

AWTR

MA WIN ART

ERIAI

MUST PLAY

Windsor Castle, Round Tower and Guards on Parade.

PLAN OF
WINDSOR
AND ETON

The map labels, reading across the plan:

BOATHOUSE COTT.

LAND STAG

THE HOME PARK

PUBLIC RECREATION GROUND

BALDWINS SHORE

TANGIER CT.

SUNBURY RD.

TANGIER LANE

CUTLERS AIT

ROMNEY LOCK ROAD

LODGE

KING EDWARD VII B470

SUN CL.

WAR MEMORIAL GARDENS

CHURCH CL.

HIGH STREET

ETON CT.

ETON SQ.

OUR LADY OF SORROW RC

KINGSTABLE S.

BROCAS ST.

WINDSOR & ETON RIVERSIDE STATION

RIVER TRIPS

WINDSOR & ETON BRIDGE

FARM YD.

DATCHED RD

CHAPTER M

BROAD WATER

RIVER ST.

THAMES AV.

PUTTING BOWLING & TENNIS

THEATRE ROYAL

THE STATE APARTMENTS

ST GEORGE'S CHAPEL

ROUND TOWER

QUEEN VICTORIA

LIME AVEN

GOSWELL RD.

CENTRAL STATION

THAMES STREET

CASTLE HILL

(entrance to) WINDSOR CASTLE

EAST TER. GDN.

WINDSOR ROYAL STATION

SHOPPING CENTRE

KING EDWARD COURT

SHOPPING CENTRE

ST ALBAN'S S.

SOUTH SLOPES

THE HOME PARK

PEASCOD STREET

WILLIAM'S ST.

BATCHELORS ACRE

MADEIRA WALK

HIGH ST.

PARK ST.

THE LONG WALK

TENNIS CENTRE

FROGMORE DRIVE

ROYAL HA GOLF C

ALMS HAUSES

OBELISK

SHEET STREET

CAMBRIDGE GATE

VICTORIA STREET

BARRACK LANE

RUSSELL ST.

VICTORIA BARRACKS

BROOK ST.

WINDSOR

CRICKET GROUND

ROAD

DAGMAR R.

KEPPEL ST.

K CL.

WALK

FROGMORE

QUEE

ANY RD.

E RD.

ONARD'S CT.

RD.

BORDER

Round Tower on William I's Motte viewed from river.

Windsor Castle.

Hampton Court Palace.

5

TOWN
WALKABOUT

Edward IV's reconstruction of Windsor Castle in the C15th, notably St George's Chapel, brought new life to the town. In Elizabethan times the air in Windsor was considered to be the sweetest and purest within 30 miles of London.

Enter Church Street, the scene of C16th poetic inspiration and C17th royal passions. William Shakespeare is said to have written the 'Merry Wives of Windsor' in the Old King's Head. King

Charles II is reputed to have purchased *Drury House* and nearby *Burford House* for the use and abode of his favourite mistress Nell Gwynn. A tunnel then conveniently connected the former with the Castle.

Why not indulge your own passion, of a culinary nature, by sampling sumptuous fare in one of the quaint and reputedly haunted restaurants.

Turn the corner into Church Lane and evoke the past through your fingertips in the brass-rubbing centre, annexed to the Church of St. John the Baptist built in 1820. Above the connecting passage a plaque commemorates the early C19th Engine House which stored the parish fire engine.

Church Street, Flower Seller.

Church Street. The house was used by King Charles II.

Guildhall.

Market Cross House.

St John the Baptist Church.

The impressive Guildhall, designed by Sir Thomas Fitch and built in 1687-89, invites closer inspection: Sir Christopher Wren, in defiance of Council sceptics, built the colums short of the ceiling of the Council Chamber. No longer a Corn Exchange, the open area is frequently used to market high quality crafts. Leaning precariously towards the Guildhall is **Market Cross House** dating from around 1687 and once connected by a tunnel to the Castle. Adjacent Queen Charlotte Street is the shortest street in England and only a few strides away from the former medieval market area of the town.

Victoria Memorial and Windsor Castle.

Opposite, the Royal Windsor Information Centre houses the Town and Crown Exhibition. Queen Victoria's statue points the way with her sceptre towards **Peascod Street** which, in medieval times, was the route to the Royal Hunting Lodge.

Shops in Peascod Street.

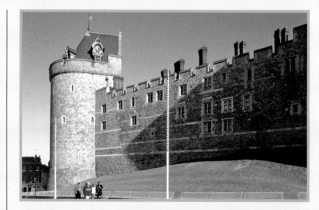

Curfew Tower. Windsor Castle Wall, West Side.

In **Curfew Yard**, in 1648, Oliver Cromwell (later Lord Protector of England) was said to have signed the death warrant of Charles I. A blocked tunnel leads from the basement to the dungeons in the Curfew Tower.

ENTERTAINMENT

Thames Street, Edward VIII's Boots Passage.

Church Street.

Windsor Thames Street.

Sir Christopher Wren's House.

White Hart Hotel.

Guarded by a bust of King Edward VIII, Boots Passage displays a tiled aerial view of Windsor Castle based on an engraving by Wenceslaus Hollar in 1663. Beyond lies Alexandra Gardens, coach park and river. Why not sojourn the night or for refreshments at **Sir Christopher Wren's House**, built by the famous architect as his family home in 1676.

Pamper yourself - wine and dine in one of Windsor's historic hotels or chic restaurants.

Indulge your fancy - purchase that special gift from quaint Church Street or from Thames Street, site of King George III's original Theatre Royal.

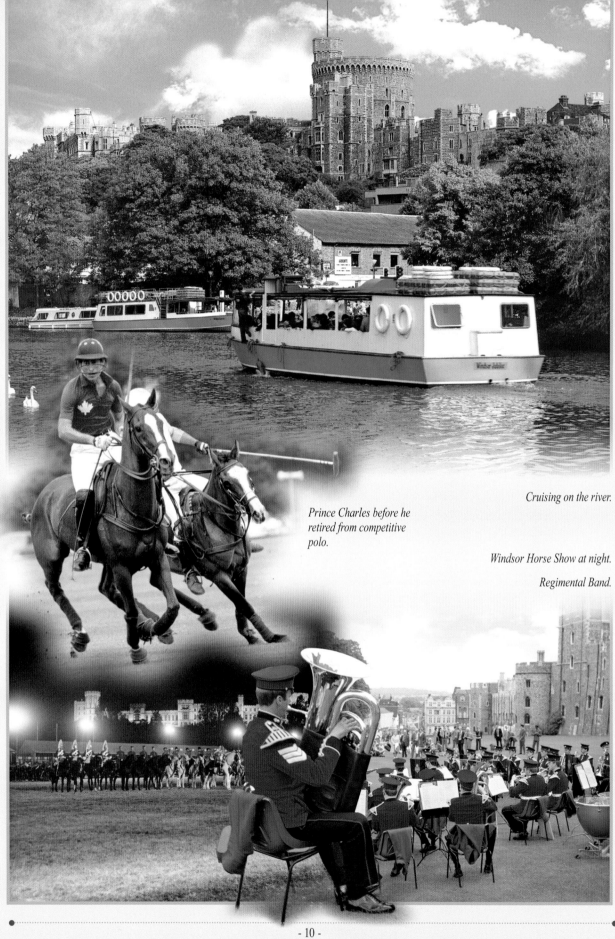

Cruising on the river.

Prince Charles before he retired from competitive polo.

Windsor Horse Show at night.

Regimental Band.

Round Tower on William I's Motte viewed from river.

RIVER THAMES

Souvenir shop, Thames Street.

Cruises may be arranged which connect with Hampton Court Palace and Runnymede, site of the historic signing of the Magna Carta in 1215.

In the reign of Henry III, water from the river, 164 feet below the present day Castle, was drawn into a well in the Round Tower possibly as a precaution in times of siege. In the more settled early C19th an ice carnival took place on the frozen river.

In contrast, in 1852, the aptly named Thames St. was flooded, impeding access to the castle.

Looking across to Eton.

Riverside restaurant.

Ready for a cruise.

Boats for hire.

THE LONG WALK AND COPPER HORSE

*'Copper Horse'.
King George III statue.*

Discover the sensory pleasure of more than 5000 acres of great Parkland, perhaps first glimpsed from the Long Walk. The prestigious 3-mile (4.5km) long treelined avenue was laid out in the reign of Charles II. Oak largely replaced original elms in Victorian times while the existing beech trees replaced diseased stock in 1942.

Unaltered by the passage of time or fashion, the Romanesque equestrian statue of King George III commands an elevated position at the end of the Long Walk on Snow Hill. George IV's memorial to his father stands 50' (15m) high from its base, the horse being large enough to accommodate sixteen people. Since the inauguration of the Ascot races by Queen Anne in 1711, horses and carriages have reverberated in royal procession down the Long Walk. Queen Victoria took the same route from Windsor Castle to her final resting-place at Frogmore.

A new award winning Visitor Centre was opened in 2006 called the Savill Building. Its modern design includes a leaf-shaped roof which appears to float above the building; its unusual design is in complete harmony with the tree line of the park. With a gallery and a restaurant it is an ideal place to begin exploring the Long Walk and the Windsor Great Park.

Windsor Castle. The Long Walk.

Windsor Castle. Round Tower with standard flying.

WINDSOR CASTLE

Windsor Castle Regimental Band.

In this new millenium Windsor Castle stands unchallenged as the largest continuously occupied castle in the world. The Castle is perched on an elongated chalk escarpment 100 feet above the River Thames. Now boasting more than 5000 acres of parkland, the royal domain once encompassed the vast Windsor Great Forest where the Normans introduced deer parks and Henry VIII enjoyed hawking and hunting wild boar and the noble stag.

During more than 900 years successive monarchs have imprinted their character upon the Castle.

William I's construction of an earthen mound or motte in the Middle Ward, housing the keep, was used by Henry II to support his Round Tower in stone. The original motte remains, the Tower being heightened and embellished for the sake of prestige in the reign of King George IV.

Windsor Castle. Curtain Wall guarding Round Tower.

Windsor Castle. Round Tower and Guards.

Upper Ward with State and Private Apartments and Statue of Charles II.

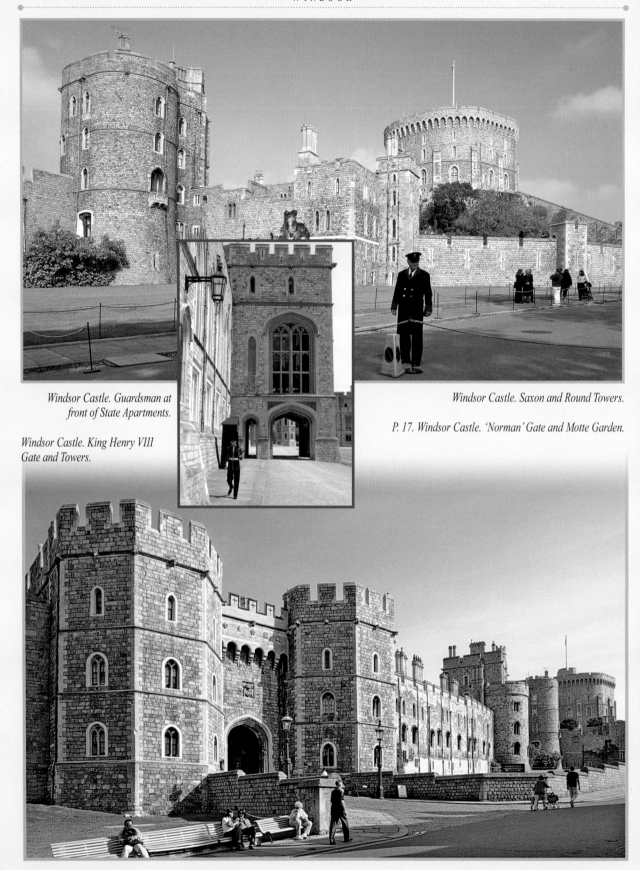

Windsor Castle. Guardsman at
front of State Apartments.

Windsor Castle. Saxon and Round Towers.

Windsor Castle. King Henry VIII
Gate and Towers.

P. 17. Windsor Castle. 'Norman' Gate and Motte Garden.

PLAN OF
THE CASTLE

Round Tower.

St. George's Chapel.

Henry VIII Gate.

Military Knights' Lodgings.

'Norman Gate'.

The Quadrangle and the statue of Charles II.

St. George's Gate.

William 'The Conqueror'.

'A man of great wisdom and power'
He was described as 'that stark man'.
Fortifications were erected in a ring around London,
and in Windsor an earthen Motte with wooden towers.

WILLIAM THE 'CONQUEROR'

(1066-1087) - (Plantagenet)

Windsor Castle, Round Tower.

T he 'Conqueror' defeated King Harold II at the Battle of Hastings in 1066, as depicted in the Bayeux Tapestry. In 1086 he ordered the 'Domesday Survey' representing the largest collection of data in Europe relating to population, land and livestock ownership in order to maximize tax revenues.

A tall, clean-shaven man, possibly of Nordic descent, William was described by his subjects as 'that stark man': the punishment for killing a stag was to suffer blinding.

William and his wife Mathilde appear to have been devoted and faithful companions.

King William's overriding concern was to consolidate his new conquest by erecting fortifications in a ring around London, within one day's march of the capital.

Windsor's chalk escarpment, rising 100 feet above the River Thames, was leased for 12 shillings a year and a new fortress of wood was built there upon a motte or artificial mound of earth.

Windsor Great Park was restocked with rabbit warrens and hares while deer were introduced to satisfy the Norman love of hunting.

Oak trees were planted as part of a new forest management to replenish wood reserves for vital construction.

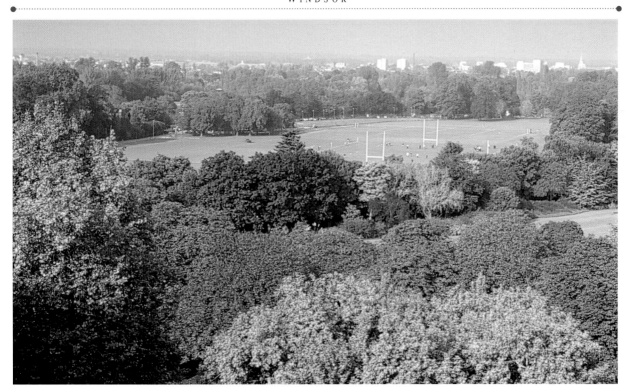

Windsor Great Forest.

Windsor Castle, Round Tower and Guards on Parade.

Henry II.

Curtain wall, Round Tower and castle were rebuilt mainly in stone. Nineteen watchtowers were erected.

HENRY II

(1154 - 1189)

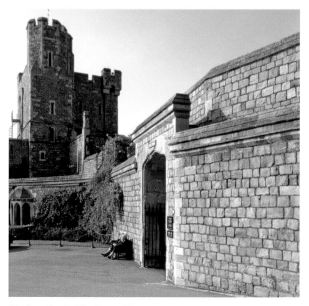

Windsor Castle. Winchester Tower.

Henry II is perhaps mainly remembered for allegedly ordering the murder of his Chancellor, Thomas Beckett, on the matter of the Church's jurisdiction over the Courts. The King's fourth and favourite son John, later King John, was responsible for sealing the Magna Carta in 1215.

Windsor Castle. Curfew Tower & Castle Wall, overlooking Thames Street.

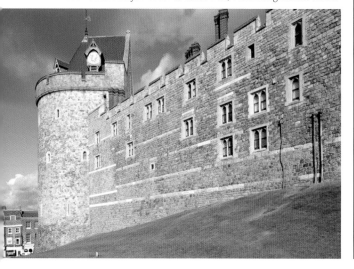

Windsor Castle's ephemeral wooden structure was rebuilt in stone, using massive boulders of resiliant heathstone dragged for miles across the former Great Windsor Forest. Prisoners held in the Curfew Tower were able to scoop out the soft chalk infilling until the very thickness of the walls defeated them.

Windsor Castle was then arranged into three baileys or Wards. Thirty feet lower than its later modified form, the Round Tower served its purpose as a keep or stronghold. A half mile long Curtain wall in stone took sixty years to complete and defended the Lower Ward. The north side of the Upper Ward, the steepest side facing the river, continued to be reserved for the family's own occupation.

Nineteen watchtowers were erected during the troublesome closing years of the monarch's reign.

Henry III.

Added 5 rounded towers in stone to Curtain wall.
Royal Chapel built on the site of Albert Memorial Chapel,
Lower Ward.

HENRY III

(1216 - 1272)

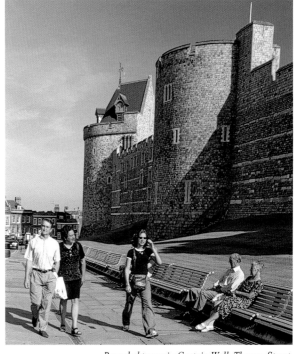

Rounded tower in Curtain Wall, Thames Street.

Only nine years old when he acceded to the throne, Henry III was the son of King John who, in 1215, had sealed the Magna Carta. He became a great patron of ecclesiastical architecture and undertook the rebuilding of Westminster Abbey. Windsor Castle was a favoured residence, his Queen Eleanor and many of their six children sojourning here for long periods. One of their daughters, Margaret, was born at the Castle.

At Windsor Castle cisterns were constructed to collect clean rain water, a well in the Round Tower connecting with the River Thames. The Castle's defences were strengthened, the west wall being repaired in stone.

Following the two sieges in connection with the feud between Henry II's sons Richard and John, five rounded

Windsor Castle, Round Tower with battlements.

towers were added in stone to the Curtain wall. The round design adopted by Richard I was less vulnerable to attack than the traditional English square structure. Queen Eleanor's comfort was improved by the addition of even more luxurious apartments in the Upper Ward, "contigious with the King's, and under the same roof".

In the Lower Ward the Royal Chapel dedicated to Edward the Confessor, was built between 1240-1248, and occupied the site of the present Albert Memorial Chapel.

Edward III.

The king expanded the building at the castle.
In the Upper Ward a Gothic Palace was arranged.
A new St George's Hall was erected.
The 'Norman Gate' separated the Upper and Lower Wards.

EDWARD III

(1327 - 1377)

His claim to Philip VI's throne of France began the so-called Hundred Years War. Edward's reign witnessed both the ravages of the Black Death and the early masterpieces of Chaucer. Possibly influenced by the romantic Legend of King Arthur and the Knights of the Round Table, Edward created the Order of the Garter, the most Noble Order of Chivalry in Europe.

Prince Edward was born at Windsor Castle and was baptized in the old Chapel of St. Edward. Following the death of his Queen, Philippa of Hainault, the King became a virtual recluse at Windsor. In stature Edward was described as tall and of impressive build. A skilled warrior, his physical attributes seem to have contributed toward his triumph at the battle of Crécy in 1346.

Edward III founded the College of St. George and the Order of the Garter at Windsor in 1348. Twenty-six Poor Knights served to pray for king

Procession of the Noble Order of the Garter.

and country on behalf of the Knights of the Garter. Every year on St. George's Day a ceremonial banquet took place using the old St. George's Hall.

Each June the present Monarch dons a cloak of dark blue velvet, the blue garter holding the emblem of the Garter Star: 'Honi soit qui mal y pense' (shame on him who thinks evil of it).

In 1348, work was begun at the Castle. King David of Scotland was ransomed for 100,000 crowns to help finance construction.

The Chapel of Edward the Confessor was extensively altered and dedicated to St. George. The misnamed 'Norman Gate', with its own portcullis, separated the Upper and Lower Wards. Edward favoured impressive Gothic architecture of pointed arches and flying butresses, a style which had been introduced by Henry III. In 1357 the Bishop of Winchester, William of Wykeham, was instructed to direct the construction of the Upper Ward. The outcome was a large Gothic Palace arranged around inner courtyards. A new St. George's Hall with an impressive arched-beam ceiling was erected between 1362-5, to house banquets for Knights of the Garter.

Windsor Castle,
'Norman Gate'.

Edward IV.

War of the Roses: more than 36,000 men were slain in one day.
Building of St George's Chapel, and New Cloisters.

EDWARD IV

(1461 - 1483)

Edward was declared King by Parliament in 1461 after defeating the Lancastrians during the war of the Roses in the bloodiest battle ever on British soil, when more than 36,000 men were slain in one day. He was deposed in 1470 and restored to the throne less than one year later.

Windsor Castle, St George's Chapel.

Windsor Castle, Dean's Cloister.

His greatest memorial is St. George's Chapel, Windsor Castle, home of the ancient Chivalrous Order of the Garter.

King Edward was reported to have had the physique of a warrior and the propensity to be pleasure seeking. He was tall and burly, his lead coffin measuring 6'3" in length. Talents included the military art, and dancing, both of which seemed to have endeared him to the ladies. He married rather furtively in 1464 the beautiful and widowed Lady Grey (née Elizabeth Woodville) who bore him 10 children.

Edward's marriage alienated influential followers, the Civil War was reopened and the King was forced for a period to flee to France.

Solar Clock, St. George's Chapel.

Whilst at Windsor the King enjoyed impressing his guests. During a reception given in honour of Lord Grutheryse, Edward presented the ambassador with a cup of gold, inlaid with pearls and sapphires. The following day's itinerary included hunting, followed by a tour of the Castle gardens and Vineyard. Evensong preceded a banquet given by the Queen at 9.00 p.m. after which a tour of the royal apartments feasted the eye. After bathing, the guest was treated to 'green ginger, divers syrups, sweets and spicy wine'.

A new St. George's Chapel was created, the finest building in the whole Castle compound. The founder is buried here, beneath a simple black stone, in the vicinity of the Cloisters for which he was also responsible.

St. George's Chapel

St. George's Chapel has been described as 'the shrine of British royalty'. Ten English Monarchs are buried here and six Queens. Here lies Henry VIII who requested to be buried in the same vault as his favourite Queen Consort, Jane Seymour. Sixteen Yeomen of the Guard of exceptional height and strength carried his massive lead coffin. The widowed Catherine Parr, Henry VIII's sixth and last wife, observed the funeral from the Queen's closet, originally designed for the first Queen Consort Catherine of Aragon. Her own emblem of pomegranates can be seen among the awe-inspiring ornamentation.

Shortly before his execution Charles I spent his last Christmas at Windsor Castle, as a prisoner. His burial was conducted in silence and without the usual pomp and ceremony on the orders of Oliver Cromwell, Lord Protector of the newly found government during the Interregnum (1649-1658). Even the location of King Charles I's tomb remained secret until 1813 when the Prince Regent (later George IV) decided to settle the issue. Where do you think he was interred? A clue may be provided by a particular stone slab on the floor of the Chapel Choir wherein lies the vault of Henry VIII.

Windsor Castle,
St. George's Chapel,
detail of King's Beasts.

Windsor Castle, St. George's Chapel, stone sculpture.

Windsor Castle, Cloister and St. George's Chapel.

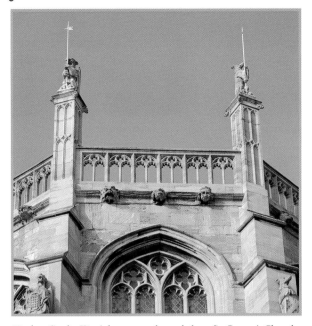

Windsor Castle, King's beasts stand guard above St. George's Chapel.

Windsor Castle. St. George's Chapel, detail of heraldic coat-of-arms.
(P. 30-31) St George's Chapel. The choir stalls.

St. George's Chapel has witnessed several royal weddings. When Queen Victoria's eldest son and heir, HRH Albert Edward, the Prince of Wales, was married to Alexandra of Denmark on 10th March 1863, she secluded herself from the scrutiny of the public in the Queen's Closet. Only one year and three months previously she had herself lost, through bereavement, her own beloved partner in marriage, her Consort Prince Albert. On the day of his engagement to Miss Sophie Rhys Jones, Prince Edward had described the Chapel as "a glorious piece of architecture" in "a wonderful setting".

A masterpiece of medieval perpendicular architecture the Chapel was built as a spiritual home for the Order of the Garter. Construction began in 1475 in the reign of Edward IV but was not completed until 50 years later in the reign of Henry VIII. The Chapel's name was inspired by King Edward III's enchantment with the legends of King Arthur and the Knights of the Round Table.

Every June the reigning monarch presides over the ceremony of the Order of the Garter, seated in an elaborately carved stall, accompanied by a fanfare of trumpets, anthems and prayers and the uplifting music of the great organ. During the Garter Ceremony in 1666 Samuel Pepys described the Chapel as "a noble place indeed". Glance upwards and capture the multi-coloured splendour of heraldic banners, crowned by the intricately carved fan-vaulted roof completed in 1528. Consider the C15th stalls in the Choir, with their boldly expressed heraldic art, displaying each Knight's coat-of-arms, crest, mantle and helm (witnessed overleaf).

Windsor Castle, King's Beast on top of St. George's Chapel.

Henry VIII.

Henry VIII Gateway, Lower Ward.
He had six wives: Catherine of Aragon, Anne Boleyn,
Jane Seymour, Anne of Cleves, Catherine Howard, Catherine Parr.

HENRY VIII

(1509 - 1547)

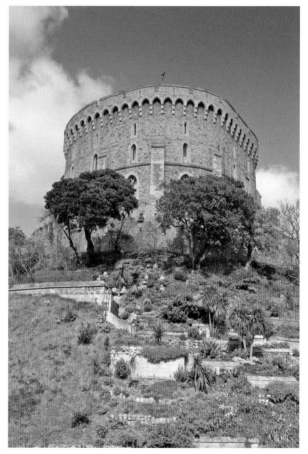

Round Tower and Garden.

Henry was the first English King to be styled 'Majesty'. He is perhaps best remembered for having had six wives, two of whom were beheaded. He met Anne Boleyn at Windsor Castle. Henry held the balance of power in Europe, defied the papacy in Rome, was responsible for the dissolution of monasteries in England, and in 1534, appointed himself the supreme Head of the Church. He was the founder of Trinity College, Cambridge. Henry fathered Mary (later Mary I) and Elizabeth (later Elizabeth I).

Henry VIII is the most famous English King. As a young man he was regarded as the most accom-plished prince of his age - handsome, athletic, a skilled hunter, capable musician and linguist. His prowess at jousting, including at Windsor, earned him the nickname 'Bluff King Hal'. Here he often did "....Ride forth on hawking or walks in the Park". His hunting sword is on display in the Queen's Chamber at Windsor Castle.

Perhaps his courtship of Anne Boleyn took place within view of the Round Tower. The King's person would be instantly recognized on arrival at the cas-tle by his large square face, red-gold beard and familiar slash and bejewelled attire. When the age-ing Henry chose the spirited Duchess of Milan for his fourth wife she was said to have not only re-fused his suit, but remarked had she two heads the King of England might be welcome to one of them - halas, she had only one.

Shortly after his marriage, in 1509, to Catherine of Aragon, Henry left his palace at Greenwich and brought the entire court to Windsor Castle. Here Garter ceremonies were lavish. Within the first year of his reign Henry ordered the construction of the impressive gateway to the Lower Ward. King Henry VIII Gateway comprises a wide arch supported on either side by massive stone towers. While the archway bears the King's symbols of portcullis, fleur-de-lis and the combined roses of Lancaster and Yorkshire, do you know the purpose of the holes in the stonework? Had you been an unwelcome visitor to Henry's court, you may have been anointed with boiling oil. The King is said to have been responsible for developing the North Terrace, now obscured by trees, which provided a panoramic view of the Thames Valley.

At Windsor Castle Henry met his second wife, Anne Boleyn, whom he espied sewing in Canon's Cloisters in the Lower Ward. Perhaps her reputedly fine eyes and youth, persuaded the King to divorce Catherine of Aragon who had, in six years of marriage, failed to bear him any living sons and heirs. When the Pope refused to grant permission for Henry to annul his first marriage, the King responded by declaring himself supreme Head of

Henry VIII Gateway.

Madame Tussauds: Henry VIII and his six wives.

Round Tower on William I's Motte viewed from the same river that transported King Henry VIII from London.

the Church. Not only were the monasteries investigated and purged of abbotts and monks, at Windsor a local popular preacher Anthony Pearson was burnt at the stake in a meadow north of the Castle.

The moment Henry heard the guns at the Tower announcing Anne's death he joined Jane Seymour, was formally betrothed the next day and married ten days later. Imagine Henry's delight when Jane produced a much longed for though sickly son and heir (later King Edward VI) and his despair when the Queen died twelve days later. Princess Mary was requested to assume the chief mourner's role at the funeral which was held at Windsor Castle.

The young King Edward VI was reputed to find the Castle cold and less comfortable than Hampton Court Palace. Henry's fourth marriage to Anne of Cleves was solemnized on 6th January 1540. Perhaps the shortest lived alliance was his marriage to Anne, which lasted only six months.

Catherine Howard, Henry's fifth wife, was reputed to be sensual and beguiling yet due to her infidelity was beheaded less than two years later.

Henry's sixth and final wife, Catherine Parr, observed his funeral from the Queen's closet, St. George's Chapel.

Henry VIII died at Whitehall in London in 1547 and was buried at Windsor. When the cortege reached Henry VIII's Gateway to the Castle, the procession stretched for more than three miles from Windsor's bridge.

Mary I (Bloody Mary).

Mary Tudor Tower
Construction of Military Knights Houses in Lower Ward.

QUEEN MARY I

(1553 - 1558)

Mary Tudor Tower.

An ardent Catholic, Mary's attempts to eradicate Protestantism, including the execution of Thomas Cranmer, Archbishop of Canterbury, earned her the nickname 'Bloody Mary'. Her marriage alliance with Spain threatened the sovereignty of England and culminated in the loss of Calais, the last remaining Continental possession.

Mary, though in poor health, was the only child to survive infancy of the union between King Henry VIII and his first wife Catherine of Aragon.

Born a congenital syphilitic, Mary endured chronic ill health, including headaches, poor eyesight and ulcerative rhinitis. The disease is believed to have been passed on by her mother who contracted it from her first husband Arthur, elder brother of King Henry.

Mary's relationship with her father was erratic. Initially considered a disappointment because of her gender, she was later given her own court.

Queen Mary honoured the terms of Henry VIII's will by constructing military Knights' lodgings in the Lower Ward at Windsor Castle. Poor Knights who had distinguished themselves as soldiers were recompensed with well-maintained accommodation.

Perhaps the greatest sadness in Mary's life was the failure of her marriage in 1554 to the Catholic Philip II of Spain. In lasting memory of their short union, the C14th belfry at Windsor Castle became Mary Tudor Tower and bears both her arms and those of her husband, King Philip II of Spain.

"When I am dead", Mary had said, "you will find the words 'Philip' and 'Calais' engraved upon my heart".

Mary Tudor Tower and Military Knights' Lodgings.

Elizabeth I.

Queen Elizabeth Terrace.
Addition of Long Gallery, now Royal Library.

ELIZABETH I

(1558 - 1603)

North Terrace Entrance.

North Terrace (Queen Elizabeth I Terrace) and 'Norman Gate'.

S he had the 'heart and stomach of a king'. Drake defeated Philip II of Spain's Armada in 1588. The American Colony of Virginia is named after the 'Virgin Queen' who never married.

Daughter of Anne Boleyn, Elizabeth was Henry VIII's strongest and healthiest child. She was said to read "now at Windsor more Greek every day than some Prebendary of this church doth read Latin in a whole week".

Dubbed 'Gloriana', Elizabeth's attire was magnificent, bejewelled and adorned with her favourite pearls against a glorious halo of red hair.

Her love of riches extended to adorning the royal beds at Windsor Castle with bed hangings and tapestries of gold and fine silk. Talented at needlework, one state visitor to the Castle enthused about a "beautifully embroidered cushion done by Queen Elizabeth herself in red and white silk".

"Although the house be cold", Windsor Castle became the winter retreat of the Queen in 1563, following the outbreak of plague in London. Here she bathed in rooms "ceiled and wainscoted with looking glass".

Warmed by great fires and entertained by gathering around her children who enacted plays, Queen Elizabeth's fondness for the theatre lead to her commissioning the revered bard William Shakespeare to write "The Merry Wives of Windsor". Shakespeare is reputed to have written the play in the King's Head, now a restaurant.

The Queen walked in the gardens, usually for an hour every day before dinner. In 1572 Elizabeth ordered the restoration of her much-loved terrace.

In 1580 Elizabeth added the Long Gallery to the State Apartments (now the Royal Library).

Charles I.

Oliver Cromwell's resolution: "The King should be prosecuted for his life as a criminal person". (1649) Charles I was buried at Windsor after execution at Whitehall.

CHARLES I

(1625 - 1649)

Referred to as the 'Martyr King', Charles was the only English monarch to be beheaded. His execution at Whitehall in London, 1649, signalled the end of monarchical rule for 51 years. King Charles I's last word on the scaffold was "Remember".

During the first summer of the king's reign, when there was an outbreak of plague, the gates of Windsor Castle were locked and the royal party departed. In 1635 by a decree of court "dust and other rubbish" was removed from the unsavoury streets of Windsor. New wells were dug in the vicinity of Market Cross House in 1637.

Charles I adopted his father's belief in 'the divine right of kings'. Three times he summoned Parliament which he then dissolved.

When the king's attempt to arrest five troublesome members of Parliament in January 1642 failed, he removed his family, troops and ammunition to Windsor.

Today enjoy the ceremonial parade of guards, in contrast to the military guards who held Charles I captive.

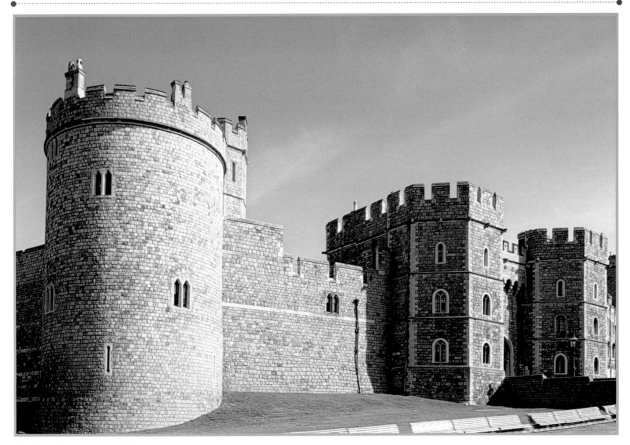

The Walls that imprisoned Charles I.

Final resting place of King Charles I.

Curfew Yard provided the setting of the fateful resolution proclaimed by Oliver Cromwell that "the King should be prosecuted for his life as a criminal person". King Charles I was accused of high treason in 1648.

He spent his last Christmas at Windsor Castle. Although he was not permitted the customary fare of mince pies and plum porridge, he could "walk where and when he pleased" and sleep in his own bed-chamber.

King Charles I's final visit to Windsor Castle was in a coffin draped with a black velvet pall. When a sudden snowstorm turned the pall white some said that Heaven had declared the King's innocence.

Charles II.

*He transformed the Upper Ward
and State Apartments in Baroque Style.
Long Walk was laid out.*

CHARLES II

(1660 - 1685)

The Restoration of the monarchy was achieved on the King's 30th birthday following 8 years in exile. The Earl of Rochester commented that "he never said a foolish thing and never did a wise one".

Yet he could not forget the demise of his father Charles I when, during his own crowning ceremony on St. George's Day 1661, he was officiated by the same Archbishop of Canterbury who had attended the Martyr King on the scaffold. In 1650 after being crowned by an act of Covenant King of Great Britain, France and Ireland he was forced to flee and hid in an oak tree, with a price of £100,000 on his head.

The Restoration of the monarchy was pro-

Dine in the house used by King Charles II, Church Street.

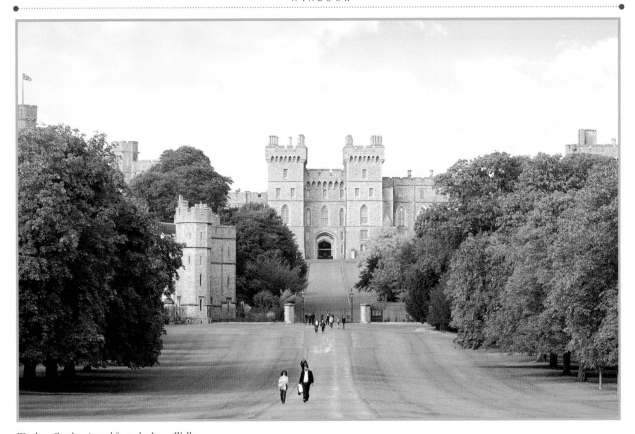

Windsor Castle, viewed from the Long Walk.

claimed in Windsor by the Mayor and Corporation "...with all joy acclamations", trumpets and drums playing. Windsor Castle became the King's summer residence and the principle palace outside London.

The architect Hugh May was charged with changing an "exceedingly ragged and ruinous" castle into a Baroque Palace. Remodelling of the State Apartments in the Upper Ward featured exquisite carvings in wood by Grinling Gibbons and huge ceiling decorations by the Italian painter Antonio Verrio. Sir Christopher Wren was appointed Surveyor General.

When the King held Court the atmosphere was pleasure seeking and marked by a languid sensuality. Verrio was appointed to decorate the stairway of the King's favourite mistress Nell Gwynn, mother of his son, the Duke of St. Albans.

Charles II created the long avenue of trees (Long Walk) being fond himself of walking as well as impressing his contemporaries. In reverence to the ancient Order of the Knights of the Garter, St. George's Chapel was restored from an internally ruinous state.

Upper Ward with State and Private Apartments and Statue of Charles II.

George III.

*Initiated Gothic reconstruction of State Apartments.
Frogmore House was acquired.*

GEORGE III

(1760 - 1820)

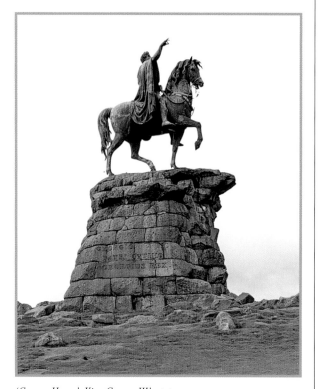

'Copper Horse', King George III's statue.

George III purchased Buckingham House (now Palace) in 1762 for £21,000 yet favoured Windsor as a royal residence.

The King moved to Windsor in 1789 on recovering from his first illness of 'porphyria', referred to as the 'royal illness'. Two of his 15 children, including his favourite Amelia, were born and died at Windsor.

In 1766 the Castle was described as "...the only place in England worthy to be styled a King's Palace (yet) so totally neglected". Queen Charlotte complained of the cold and draughts in the medieval Castle. Queen's Lodge was built to afford greater comfort, but later demolished by their son George IV who preferred an unimpeded view of the Long Walk. Today George III surveys his former Kingdom astride his mount, known as the 'Copper Horse'.

Windsor Castle, detail of Gothic reconstruction, State Apartment.

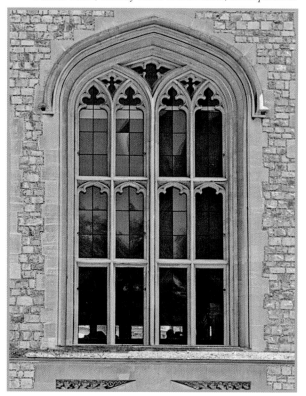

James Wyatt was appointed to Gothicize Charles II's Baroque additions. The present Grand Vestibule was a staircase in the late C18th, and retains the original elegant plaster fan-vaulted ceiling executed by Francis Bernasconi. George III's attraction for a lightened decorative appearance lead to the oak wall panels in the King's Drawing Room being replaced with bright blue damask. What enlightened spirits the guests to the Queen's ballroom must have experienced, dancing beneath the finest examples of English glass chandeliers commissioned by George III. Frogmore House in Home Park was purchased. The King became known as 'Farmer George' because of his interest in Flemish and novel methods of farming.

The King's involvement with the trade and politics of the borough and familiarity with the townspeople earned him the nickname 'Squire of Windsor'. Fanny Burney, a famous novelist at the time wrote, "He knew something of the character and affairs of most persons who live under the shadow of the Castle". The public was rewarded by having regular access to the State Apartments of the Upper Ward and precincts. According to Miss Burney promenading on the South Terrace was popular since "...all Windsor and its neighbourhood poured in upon it, to see the prince" and the King who looked "so proud of his son". He spent the final years at Windsor Castle.

Peascod Street, George III 'Squire of Windsor'.

George IV.

*Gothicized facade. Round Tower heightened.
Remodelling of State Apartments.
New Royal Apartments and Grand Corridor added.*

GEORGE IV

(1820 - 1830)

Upper Ward showing Gothic pointed arched windows.

Windsor Castle, Round Tower.

James Wyatt) to continue the Gothic transformation of the Castle. His instructions were to "do everything in a substantial manner, and not merely vamp the building". The original estimate of £150,000 eventually exceeded £1 million.

Keen to improve the silhouette of the Castle, Henry II's Round Tower was raised by 33 feet. Extra towers and battlements were constructed. The knighted Sir Jeffry was said to have "....found a crumbling ruin and left the nation with a palace".

The Duke of Wellington described him as "...the most extraordinary compound of talent, wit, buffoonery, obstinacy and good feelings".

While at banquets at the Castle he fancied himself having been present at the Battle of Waterloo. The Royal Collection at Windsor houses some of George IV's personal collection of finest china.

The King chose Jeffry Wyatville (nephew of

Waterloo Chamber.

King George IV took up residence in the Castle in 1828.

The King's fascination with the Battle of Waterloo led to the creation of the Waterloo Chamber, which commemorates the allied defeat of Napoleon. Measuring 180 feet (55 metres) in length, St. George's Hall was created by Wyatville. Stepping into the Grand Reception Room is to experience the King's preference for C18th French panelling and gilded ornamentation. Formerly a ballroom, the Queen now meets her guests here as a prelude to State banquets. In the principal semi-state room, aptly named the Crimson Drawing Room, George IV was personally responsible for the choice of the rich crimson, silk damask wall covering (restored since the fire of 1992 and shown overleaf).

Queen Victoria.

Her Consort, Prince Albert, dies at Windsor.
Restoration Lower Ward.
Grand staircase to State Apartments rebuilt.

QUEEN VICTORIA

(1837 - 1901)

The 'Widow of Windsor' was the last Hanovarian sovereign. Herself the granddaughter of George III, four future sovereigns are related to Queen Victoria: Edward VII, George V, Edward VIII and George VI. In 1876 she became Queen-Empress of India.

At Windsor Castle, in the Blue Closet, she exercised a sovereign's prerogative and proposed marriage to her cousin, Albert of Saxe-Coburg-Gotha. The christening of her eldest son Edward (later Edward VII) took place within the splendour of St George's Chapel. Three of her children were married at the Castle. Queen Victoria chose to be buried in a mausoleum at Frogmore within the grounds of Windsor Park, and alongside her Consort Prince Albert, instead of in the royal Tomb-house constructed by George III.

During her reign the staterooms were used for entertaining Heads of State from around the World and Empire, including Napoleon III. The huge malachite urn in the Grand Reception Room was given by Tsar Nicholas I.

In 1851 Victoria's greatness was acknowledged by the Maharajah of Travancore's present of an Indian Ivory throne, which can now be marvelled at in the Queen's Grand Chamber. Queen Victoria still presides over the Grand Vestibule, her royal presence epitomised in marble by Joseph Boehm in 1871.

Queen Victoria's granite statue, erected in 1887, commemorates the 50th anniversary of her reign.

Queen Victoria arranged for Anthony Salvin to realign the Grand Staircase in 1866, for the sake of convenience. A Victorian addition is the conical roof to the Curfew Tower. A more personal remembrance of the Queen is the Albert Memorial Chapel. Situated to the east of St George's, the disused Wolsey Chapel was remodelled in marble and mosaic.

Statue of Queen Victoria and Windsor Castle.

Albert Memorial Chapel. Interior.

Lower Ward and Albert Memorial Chapel.

When Prince Albert died at the Castle on 14th December 1861, possibly of typhoid fever from unsafe drains, Victoria became a familiar figure dressed in mourning black. A virtual recluse, she no longer took tea occasionally with local commoners.

Visit Windsor by train, in the shadow of Queen Victoria and the 'Royal' coach.

Queen Elizabeth II.

2012 sees the Queen celebrate her 60th Diamond Jubilee with her four children and eight grandchildren. Her remarkable reign, which has stretched over a vast period of change, is second only to Queen Victoria's in length

QUEEN ELIZABETH II

(1952 -)

The Queen became Head of the Commonwealth in 1953. In 1977, during her Silver Jubilee year, she undertook a 56,000-mile tour of Commonwealth countries. Today the Queen plays a more strenuous role in the life of the nation than her predecessors.

Queen Elizabeth represents the House of Windsor. During the First World War King George V found it propitious to create the new Dynasty of Windsor, thereby affirming his allegiance of loyalty to the town and country.

During the Second World War the Princesses Elizabeth and Margaret were evacuated from London to Windsor along with more than 3,000 other children. To help keep up their spirits they joined with members of the royal household in performing pantomimes in the Castle's Waterloo Chamber. Two of their dolls, presented by the children of France in 1938, are on display in Queen Mary's Doll house. At Windsor the future Queen learned to drive a heavy lorry in aid of the war effort.

Five years before ascending the throne in 1952 the Queen was given the Honorary Freedom of the royal Borough of Windsor. Her Majesty responded "...I regard (Windsor) as home in a

The Queen Elizabeth II.

way no other place can be". Today the royal family regularly spend their private weekends at the Castle. Until very recently the Queen continued to enjoy riding at the Royal Lodge. Many members of the Royal family share her passion for horses. Prince Philip competed in the internationally renowned Windsor Horse Show and Prince Charles also used to regularly compete in polo matches at Smiths' Lawn.

Every June the Garter Throne Room, with its carved and gilt throne canopy, witnesses the Queen's investiture of new Knights and Ladies of the Order of the Garter. Following the tradition of her ancestors, Queen Elizabeth holds ceremonial banquets for visiting Heads of State who may later find themselves sleeping in one of the reputedly capacious four-poster beds!

Windsor Castle, fire.

THE *FIRE* OF *1992*

AND ITS *RESTORATION*

Windsor Castle, St. George's Hall showing fire damage.

WINDSOR CASTLE TODAY

In 1992 a fire raged for 15 hours badly damaging Windsor Castle. The initial spark ignited a curtain in the private chapel of the Upper Ward, spreading fire through the organ and into the roof space. Nine major state rooms were damaged and the Queen later proclaimed 1992 her "annus horribilis".

A £40 million five-year restoration project returned the Castle to its former glory. The restoration was completed on the Queen's 50th wedding anniversary. The Queen is said to have remarked that the restoration of Windsor Castle was the best anniversary present she could have wished for. The Crimson Drawing Room, was completely restored and Wyatville's original hanging ceiling pinned to prevent the chandelier from swaying. St George's Hall now boasts the largest oak hammerbeam roof to have been constructed in the 20th century. Wyatville's flat plaster ceiling having collapsed, the new appearance is lighter and complements the heraldic decoration of shields representing every Garter Knight created. The redesigned private chapel of the Royal Family commemorates the fire of 1992 in a specially commissioned stained glass window.

Windsor Castle today remains as the oldest and largest inhabited castle in the world but the castle is also a functioning royal home and an important place for royal family events. In 1999 Prince Edward married Sophie Rhys-Jones in St. George's Chapel at Windsor Castle. Prince Charles was also due to marry his second wife Camilla Parker Bowles at a civil ceremony at Windsor Castle; after the wedding service a further religious blessing was planned to take place at St. George's Chapel where his younger brother Edward had married. However, under English law because the performing of a civil marriage ceremony at Windsor Castle would have meant that the venue would then have had to be made available to all members of the public wishing to be married there, Prince Charles' and Camilla Parker Bowles' wedding had

Crimson Room. Detail of restored ceiling.

Crimson Room. Detail of curtains with tassels.

to be subsequently changed to the town hall of the town of Windsor, Windsor Guildhall. The Queen and Duke of Edinburgh attended the service of blessing and held a reception for the newly-weds in Windsor Castle but did not attend the marriage ceremony itself. The Queen's absence from the civil marriage ceremony was undoubtedly due to her position as Supreme Governor of the Church of England.

Around five hundred people live and work in the castle. Although Windsor Castle is normally used by the Queen as her weekend home, it is also increasingly being used for state banquets and official entertaining in much the same fashion as Buckingham Palace. The Castle may be a working palace but it still honours important royal traditions and recalls its glorious past. For example, when the Queen is in residence the Changing of the Guard ceremony, or Guard Mounting as it is otherwise known, takes place daily except on Sundays.

St. George's Hall.

WINDSOR BRIDGE

The River Thames divides the towns of Windsor and Eton. Henry VIII and his spectacular cavalcade crossed here for the Castle in procession to celebrate the Garter Ceremony. Then the river was traversed by a wooden bridge. Today's cast-iron bridge, designed by Charles Hollis, was opened in 1850.

In gratitude to Joseph Taylor of Eton the bridge toll, allowed by Act of Parliament to recoup the great expense, was revoked in 1898.

Charles II is said to have frequented the 'Cock Pit' in Eton High Street which dates from Saxon times. In 1815 news of the Duke of Wellington's Victory at the Battle of Waterloo was first proclaimed in Eton.

Windsor Bridge.

Cock Pit, Eton High Street.

Windsor Bridge viewed from the river.

ETON COLLEGE

E ton College is arguably the most well-known school in the world. Famous Etonians have included twenty Prime Ministers, the Duke of Wellington, George Orwell (author and political satirist) and Shelley, famous poet and husband of Mary Shelley who wrote the novel 'Frankenstein'. How would you recognise an Etonian by his uniform? In the late C18th the costume was described as consisting of "black cloaks or gowns, a square hat or cap.", still recognisable today!

Eton College.

Eton College has survived the vicissitudes of time and the whims of monarchs. When Edward IV, temporarily ousted King Henry VI and became king in 1461, work on the college initially halted until William Westby, the Provost, persuaded the new King not to dissolve the institution. Neither the College nor the Provost however had the power to prevent the arrival of the Great Western railway in 1848, the Provost fearing his boys would be corrupted by having speedy and easy access to London.

In March 1882, two Etonians helped to thwart the assassination attempt on Queen Victoria.

Eton College Forecourt and Henry VI statue .

Traditional Eton College Outfitters.

Henry VI laid the foundation stone in 1441. Etonians were intended to succeed to Oxford and Kings College Cambridge. On the anniversary of the King's death representatives of Eton and Kings College place white roses on his tomb in St George's Chapel. The King had made special provision for free schooling and accommodation for at least seventy underprivileged boys, from any part of the world. His original design of the chapel would have equalled that of St. Paul's. During Henry VIII's reign, his apparent meanness was recorded. Although the College on one occasion spent £18 entertaining the King, Henry in return sought fit only to give 13s 14d to the church and £3 6s 8d for all the masters and pupils.

Hampton Court Palace.

Hampton Court Palace, Clock Court.

HAMPTON COURT PALACE

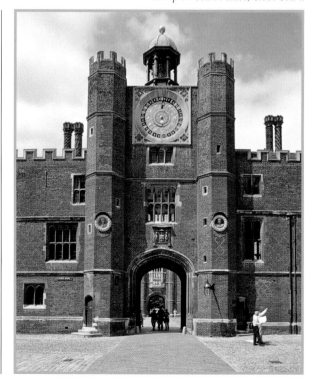

Situated beside the River Thames, Hampton Court Palace lies 13 miles upstream from London. This has been a royal residence since the C16th and the reign of King Henry VIII. Today the National Trust invites visitors on costumed guided tours to explore the treasures of our heritage.

Cardinal Wolsey, chief advisor and confidant for 16 years to the young King Henry VIII, leased the original Saxon manor for £50 per annum from the 'Knights Hospitallers'.

Great Kitchen.

Hampton Court Palace, Tudor Kitchens.

Hampton Court Palace comprising 1000 rooms, a Great Hall, Chapel and audience rooms all decorated with tapestries of gold and crimson thread and adorned with silver and gold plate, currently valued at £1 million. Living was made comfortable with silk upholstery and carpets brought from the East by Venetian merchants. At a cost of £50,000 clean water was piped from a spring 3 miles away. The 2000 acres of parkland were stocked with deer.

When, in June 1525, King Henry VIII asked Wolsey why he had built such a magnificent palace, the Cardinal was said to cleverly reply, "To show how noble a palace a subject may offer to his sovereign".

Inspite of Wolsey having been described by a Venetian ambassador as "seven times greater than the Pope", he was obliged to transfer the lease of Hampton Court Palace to the King in an ill-fated attempt to retain the King's favour.

Henry's first wife, Catherine of Aragon, visited the palace during divorce proceedings in January 1529. Anne Boleyn spent her honeymoon here in 1533, pregnant with the future Queen Elizabeth I.

The Chapel was lavishly redecorated. Look skyward to the faithfully restored azure blue ceiling, the gold stars being a sentimental Victorian idea. Although little remains of Henry's apartments, Jane Seymour and the beheaded 5th wife, Catherine Howard, are said to haunt the Queen's Apartments and Upper Gallery. At Hampton Court the future King Edward VI, Henry's only legitimate surviving male heir, was born on 12th October 1537. Jane, Henry's favourite wife, died 12 days later following his birth.

When walking through the Great Kitchen imagine the smells and tastes of the adjacent bakeries, sauceries, meat and poultry kitchens and wine cellar. Children turned the spits carrying whole wild boar and deer.

A larger Great Hall was erected measuring 160' long, 40' wide and 60' high.

Hampton Court Palace, Wine Cellar.

For entertainment, Henry introduced indoor tennis from France. In the parterre garden of formal hedges Henry courted Catherine Howard, immediately following his divorce from the 4th wife, Anne of Cleves.

Mary Tudor honeymooned at the Palace with her groom Philip II of Spain. Princess Elizabeth was held in custody by Mary, returning as Queen to the Palace for rest and quiet, working in the gardens for 1 hour each morning. Exotic plants were brought from abroad by Raleigh and Hawkins. William Shakespeare performed plays here. The eligible Elizabeth received marriage proposals and plans at the Palace, but rejected them all.

Queen Elizabeth's successor, King James I of England and Scotland, hosted the conference of the so-called "Millenary Petition" in 1604: Puritan demand for simplified religious observance.

During the Civil War King Charles II was impris-

Hampton Court Palace Parterre Garden.

oned at the Palace, escaping via a private passage to the Water Gallery (where princess Elizabeth had previously been imprisoned).

Following the King's execution, Oliver Cromwell, Lord Protector of the Commonwealth, lived here simply and economically.

When Charles II acceded to the throne in 1660 Louis XIV's landscape gardener was borrowed to restructure the formerly flat parkland.

Hampton Court Palace and Privy Gardens.

Sir Christopher Wren was commissioned by King William III to build a rival to Louis XIV's palace at Versailles. Rectangular massive structures redolant of the French Renaissance replaced most of the Tudor haphazard skyline. Antonio Verrio's painted ceiling and walls still adorn the King's Grand Staircase.

George II and Queen Caroline were the last two British Sovereigns to actually live in the Palace. The grounds were further reshaped by the later famous 'Capability Brown'.

William IV restored Hampton Court to its former glory. Unfortunately, on Easter Monday 1986, fire destroyed much of the south range of Wren's Fountain Court. A policy of 'total salvage' restored 75 per cent of the original oak panelling and 64 per cent of the original mouldings.

Hampton Court Palace, Fountain Court.

LEGOLAND

Legoland, main entrance.

T he domain of Legoland beckons within a short journey from Windsor.

At Legoland, children of all ages from grandchildren to grandparents can be creative, have fun, develop the imagination, play and learn in an exciting yet safe environment. With two major roller coasters and six water rides Legoland is a world of adventure for all ages. Allow your imagination free reign while exploring Miniland with its scaled replica of famous London sights and the aptly named Imagination Theatre which now houses a state-of-the-art 4D cinema.

Legoland is full of surprises. There are stunt shows which vie for your attention and water attractions which are guaranteed to capture the imagination. The Atlantis Submarine Voyage is an absolutely unique magical underwater experience. Take the plunge with this world first lego submarine adventure: a journey to the bottom of the sea where you can spot lego models while searching for the ancient ruins of Atlantis. Legoland also caters for those who seek a few moments of quietude and relaxation in the Enchanted Forest.

Need to give that imagination of yours a rest or just ravenous? The Park has a number of eating places which cater for all tastes and pockets.

Legoland, Buckingham Palace

Legoland, Tower Bridge.

The Splendour of
WINDSOR
ETON, HAMPTON COURT AND LEGOLAND

Graphics: Storti Edizioni S.r.l.
Text: Danuta Balcerowska
BA (HON.) London University
Text revised and up-dated by Maria McQuillan

THOMAS BENACCI LTD
Unit 12 Bessemer Park
250 Milkwood Road
Herne Hill - London SE24 OHG
Tel. 020 7924 0635
Fax 020 7924 0636
www.thomasbenacci.co.uk
sales@thomasbenacci.co.uk

Photography: Powel Libera
(a = above; c = center; b = below; l = left; r = right)
• *'The Royal Collection* © *2000, Her Majesty Queen Elizabeth II':* **John Freeman** *pages 19ar - 30/31 - 51ar;* **Mark Fiennes** *pages 47- 48/49- 55.*
• *'The National Portrait Gallery London':*
pages 20 - 22 - 23 - 24 - 26 - 32 - 36 - 38 - 40 - 42 - 44 - 46 - 50 - 52.
• *www.shutterstock.com/Lee Torrens page 4cbl, 43a;* **/Filip Fuxa** *page 11a,35;* **/Chrislofoto** *page 13b, 50;* **/Mike Liu** *page 18a,32cr;* **/Bobo Ling** *page 18b;* **/St. Nick** *page 25;* **/Jon le-bon** *page 33;* **/Sunxuejun** *page 37;* **/Evgeny Murtola** *page 43b;* **/J. Helgason** *page 56-57;* **/Alexander Dashewsky** *page 58b;* **/Stephen Mulcahey** *front cover flap (al);* **/Jeni Foto** *front cover flap (cl);* **/trappy76** *front cover flap (cr);* **/J. Helgason** *back cover flap (al);* **/Chrislofoto** *back cover flap (cr).*
• *The* **SKYSCAN Photo Library***: Air picture pages 2/3.*
• *Ag. Grazia Neri: page 34.*
• *Tim Rooke/Rex Feature: page 53.*
• *David Levenson / Colorific: page 54.*
• *Wikipedia (Cherryguy93): Legoland pages 4bl- 63cb*

CONTENTS

Plan of Windsor and Eton 5
Town Walkabout 6
Entertainment 9
River Thames 11
The Long Walk and 'Copper Horse' 13
Windsor Castle 14
Plan of the Castle 18
William the 'Conqueror' 20
Henry II 22
Henry III 23
Edward III 24
Edward IV 26
St George's Chapel 28
Henry VIII 32
Queen Mary I 36
Elizabeth I 38
Charles I 40
Charles II 42
George III 44
George IV 46
Queen Victoria 50
Queen Elizabeth II 52
The Fire of 1992 and its restoration 54
Windsor Castle today 54
Windsor Bridge 58
Eton College 59
Hampton Court Palace 60
Legoland 63

Cover:
Windsor Castle. Round Tower and Guards.